PILLARS OF THE SLAVIC CHURCH

Letter and Donations of Louis II the German

Louis II the German
King of East Francia

Translated by: D.P. Curtin

Dalcassian Publishing Company
PHILADELPHIA, PA

Copyright @ 2009 Dalcassian Publishing Company

All rights reserved. No part of this publication may be reproduced, distributed, or transmitted in any form or by any means, including photocopying, recording, or other electronic or mechanical methods, without the prior written permission of the publisher, except in the case of brief quotations embodied in critical reviews and certain other non-commercial uses permitted by copyright law. For permission request, write to Dalcassian Publishing Company at dalcassianpublishing at gmail.com

ISBN: 979-8-8692-6819-8 (Paperback)

Library of Congress Control Number:
Author: Curtin, D.P. (1985-)

Printed by Ingram Content Group, 1 Ingram Blvd, La Vergne, Tennessee

First printing edition 2009.

LETTER I

In the name of the Lord God and our Savior Jesus Christ: Louis and Lothair, by divine providence, are the Emperors of Augustus. If, in the manner of the emperor, we are bestowing upon the places which are subject to the worship of the gods, we are bestowing on them convenient benefits, we have no doubt that this will contribute to the stability of our empire and the health of our souls. Therefore, we want it to be known to all the faithful of the holy church of God and ours, present and future, that at the request of our beloved son Louis, King of Bavaria and Count Gerold, we have granted a certain monastery to ours, the name of which is Chremisa, which was built in honor and veneration of our Lord and Savior The site of Jesus Christ in the village of Trungowe, where at the present time the venerable man Sigehard the abbot is in charge, and the monks have lived there for a long time. was paid to the count, where also the monks of the aforesaid monastery built a church and a house and other buildings. That territory is thus delimited. For it begins from the eastern side of Sumerperoch, as the messengers of Count Gerold have pointed out, as far as Draeisma to the place called Hohoga Plaettchinn, and from there upwards to the territory of the episcopate of the Patavian church and from there to the southern side as far as Heribrunnum. Then from the western side to the place where Flinspach comes out of the forest on the northern side, as the forest itself continues as far as the already mentioned mountain, which is called Sumerperch.

The mentioned territory, however much it consists of the above-mentioned delimitation, saving the property of free slaves, the rest whatever below these delimitations at the present time belonged to the part of the count, we hand over all to the aforesaid monastery of Chremisa by this authority of ours, and by our right transfer it to its right and dominion, so to speak , so that whatever the governors and ministers of the aforesaid monastery may wish to do or judge for the benefit and progress of the aforesaid territories, they may have free will in all things to do whatever they choose. And in order that this authority may be able to remain unshaken under the protection of our lord in future times, we have confirmed it with our own hands and ordered it to be sealed with the impression of our ring...

I recognized Durandus the deacon at the turn of Fridagis. Given in the month of April on the 11th. In the year of Christ's propitiation XV. The sixth year of the reign of Lord Louis the Most Serene Emperor, and Lothar. Indictment VI. Act of the Aachen Palace in the name of God. Amen.

LETTER II

In the name of our Lord Jesus Christ, God Almighty. Louis, by divine grace, king of the Bavarians. ... the venerable man Gauzbaldus, chief chaplain of our sacred palace and abbot of the monastery called Altaha, which was built in honor of St. Maurice, the martyr of Christ, coming and acquainting our excellency with our clemency, how after the land of the Avars had been partially taken by our grandfather, the emperor Charles, with his permission and consent certain things belonging to the right of the king in the march itself would have been granted to the same monastery, which even until now the aforesaid monastery possessed. But since the authority of the tradition was not at all apparent, the same abbot Gauzbald begged us to grant him the gift and confirmation of our authority to the monastery, by means of which he would be able to hold and dominate the very things in the aforesaid monastery and its governors without any hindrance or contradiction. To whose supplication, for the sake of divine love and reverence for the holy place itself, we willingly nod, and by a solemn donation granted the same things to be permanently possessed by the monastery, that is, the place called Uuahouua, which ends from the source of the river called Mustrica to the place where the Danube itself flows, and then it stretches up to the bank of the Danube as far as Bohbab, and beyond Bohbah one land, and from there by Bohbah up to the top of the mountain which is called Ahornico, and also another place called Accussabah near the bank of the Danube, the measure of which is one mile in length and likewise in breadth, nor even one field, which contains one manor, which is interposed by the cause of the Frisian church. Therefore, these things, together with the manors, houses, buildings, vineyards, lands, forests, meadows, pastures, waters, or streams, regardless of the extent to which the aforesaid boundaries concerning the same things are contained, we assign the whole and entire to the right and dominion of the predestinate of the church in perpetuity; so that whatever the governors and ministers of the aforesaid see may wish to do or judge about themselves or in themselves for the benefit and convenience of the church itself, they may have free power in all things to do whatever they choose...

Adalleodus the deacon recognized Gauzbald's advice.

First of October in the year of Christ, the propitiation of the 17th year of the reign of Lord Louis, the Serene Augustus, and in the 5th year of our reign, the 7th indictment. Act of the state of Ragenesburg. Amen.

LETTER III

In the name of our Lord Jesus Christ, God Almighty. Louis, by the generous grace of God, king of the Bayorians... we, for our reward, have granted the increase of the church of St. Reginesburg, which was built in honor of St. Peter, prince of the apostles, and St. Emmeramma, where also the same blessed martyr rests buried in the body of Christ, to whom at the present time the venerable man Baturic The bishop seems to be presiding over certain things of our property, which are in the province of the Avars, that is, the place where there was an ancient castle, called Herlungoburg, with the rest of the adjoining districts, the boundaries of which are from the place where the Erlafa falls into the Danube, upwards through the bank of the same river as far as the place called Erdgastegi, and from the same river on the eastern side to the middle mountain called Colomezza near Winades, where evident signs are shown in two trees, and so on at that place on the north side to the Danube and to the south and west through the top of the mountain, as evidenced by the signs of the trees, as far as the aforesaid place of Erdgastegi. These things, therefore, with the Slavs, which are common there with houses, buildings, cultivated and uncultivated lands, meadows, pastures, woods, waters, and streams adjacent to accessible exits and regresses, regardless of the extent to which the aforesaid boundaries are contained, we have granted to the aforesaid church forever to have the whole and to the whole, and by our right into the right and dominion We have contributed to his liberality, so that from this day and time, whatever the governors and ministers of the said see may wish to do or judge for the benefit and convenience of the same church, from this day and time forward, they may enjoy free discretion to do whatever they choose...

Adalleodus, the deacon, recognized and subscribed to Gauzbaldi's advice.

Given on the 2nd of October in the 18th year of the reign of Lord Louis, the Serene Augustus, and in the 7th year of our reign, by the 11th indictment; an act of the city of Regensburg; in the name of God, happily, amen.

LETTER IV

In the name of our Lord Jesus Christ the Almighty God. Louis, by the divine grace, King of Bavaria, granted to us, as a reward for our increase, the church of Pataui, which was built in honor of St. Stephen the protomartyr, where also St. Valentinus, the confessor of Christ, rests in the body of Christ, over whom at the present time the venerable man Reginarius, the bishop, seems to preside over certain things of our property, that they are in the province of the Auars, in a place called Litaha above a spring called Sconibrunn, which Theoderic once had in his power. Therefore, these things, as we have said, with houses, houses, cultivated land, and uncultivated meadows, forests, pastures, waters, and watercourses, adjacent to accessible exits and regresses, all and in their entirety, as the aforesaid Theoderic had them in his power, so we granted to the aforesaid church presentarily, and of our right in right and we confer the dominion of his liberality on our office, so that whatever the governors and ministers of the aforesaid see choose to do with regard to the matters themselves according to ecclesiastical law, they may enjoy free will in all things to do, so much so that as long as Anno archbishop and Anno his nephew have arrived, they may hold and use the same things and no one presumes to abstract them from them, and after their departure they return with integrity to the same excellency...

Adalleodus the deacon recognized Gauzbald's advice.

Given on the 4th of March. in the 20th year of the reign of Lord Louis the Serene Augustus, and in the 7th year of our reign, by the 11th indictment. The act of Ostrehoua to our palace; m in the name of God, happily, amen.

LETTER V

In the name of the holy and individual trinity. Louis, by the divine grace of the king... for our reward we granted an increase to the church of Patauensis, which was built in honor of St. Stephen the protomartyr, where also St. Valentinus, the confessor of Christ, rests in the body of Christ, over which at the present time the venerable man Reginarius the bishop seems to be presiding over certain things of our property, which are in the province of the Aurors, in a place called Kirichbach, that is, a church built together with a territory to make a hundred mansos and more, the boundaries of which are from the same place going along one path to the place called (Mound) and thence roundabout as far as the aforesaid Kirichbach and thence to the mark of Theotheril and thence up to Cumenberg. These things, therefore, when the aforesaid church, with its vineyards, cultivated and uncultivated lands, meadows, woods, pastures, waters, and watercourses, accessible to the exits and regresses, all and in their entirety, just as Ratbodus, count of Annoni, consigned the very things to the archbishop, so we granted to the aforesaid church for the time being, and from our right into the right and dominion We grant him the gift of our liberality, so that whatever the governors and ministers of the aforesaid see wish to do with regard to the matters themselves according to ecclesiastical law, they may enjoy free will in all things to do, namely, so long as Anno archbishop and Anno his nephew have arrived, they may hold and use the same things and no one He presumes to withdraw himself from them, and after their departure they return with integrity to the same church.

The deacon Adalieus recognized Grimaldi's advice and signed it.

Dated the 14th of March in the year of Christ the propitiation of the third reign of the lord Louis, king in eastern France, by the indictment of the XIV. The act of Ostrenhoua, the palace of the region; in the name of God, happily, amen.

LETTER VI

In the holy and individual name of the Trinity. Lödewicus, by the divine favor of the king... We, as a reward for our increase, granted the church of Juuau, which was built in honor of St. Peter, the prince of the apostles, where also St. Redbert, the confessor, rests buried in the body of Christ. a certain territory in Sclauinia in a place called Ipusa near Ipusa fumen—on both sides of the river it is bounded from the western side, which is called the Theodiscan language of Wagreini, to the eastern side to one small stream, from the aguilonal side of that state to the middle of the river. Therefore, this territory with the soclesia, which Adalram once built there according to our license, with fields, forests, meadows, pastures, waters, and watercourses, movable and immovable, contained in the same way as the aforesaid boundaries, we have granted to the church in whole and in its entirety... and whatever the ministers of the aforesaid see for the benefit and convenience of the church choose to do or decide, they shall be free... to enjoy the discretion of doing whatever they choose...

Adalleod, the deacon, recognized Grimaldi's advice and signed it.

Dated on the 8th of the month of October in the propitious year of Christ, the fourth of the reign of Lord Louis, king in eastern France, by the 15th indictment. Acts given in Ohoberg; in the name of God, happily, amen.

LETTER VII

In the name of the holy and individual trinity. Hludouicus, by the divine grace of the king, ... we, having spoken to our faithful, the venerable bishop of Baturic, the count of Uuermharius, the count of Baboni, that we had arranged to grant some things of our property to a certain presbyter named Dominicus for our own, which we did so, in the place which is said to Brunnaron, which encompassed Ratpero, the cleric of Tuxta, a brook called Seuira in the Marche, where the counties of Radpoti and Rihharu border, among woods, fields, meadows, pastures, water, or streams, or whatever the aforesaid Ratpero cleric was surrounded by, we granted to the same presbyter Dominicus for our alms...

Reginbertus the subdeacon recognized and subscribed to the advice of Radlaic.

Act at Rotachin on the 17th of the month of October in the year Christ propitiation of the 12th reign of Lord Louis, king in eastern France; in the name of God, happily, amen.

LETTER VIII

In the name of the holy and individual trinity. King Louis, by divine favor, ... the venerable man Gozbald, bishop of the church of Wurzburg, coming to our presence, presented something to our blind men. the commandment of our lord and father of the piety of the memory of the most serene Augustus of Louis, in which was contained, how richly remembered lord Charles and our most excellent grandfather the emperor had commanded his predecessors Bereuuelpho and Liudrido and Egiluardo and also Wolfgarius the bishops, so that in the land of the Slavs, who sit between Moin and Radantia rivers, which are called Moinuuinids and Ratanzuurmnids, together with the counts who were appointed over the same slaves, they had arranged for churches to be built there as in other Christian places, in so far as that people could have been newly converted to Christianity, where they could receive baptism and hear preaching and where a divine office could have been celebrated among them as among other Christians; and thus by the aforesaid bishops and counts, who at that time had been in charge of the same people, he asserts that it was completed, and that fourteen churches were built there. In addition, our lord and father the most pious emperor... to endow the aforesaid basilicas, which, as we have said, were built by the aforesaid bishops in the land of the aforesaid slaves by the order and advice of our lord Charles or our grandfather, in the same village, he handed over from his own property to one of the remaining two with the remaining two to be taxed, with the exception of that manor, on which each of the churches was originally built, he granted and confirmed inviolably to have it in full forever, in such a way that whatever the same taxpayers have to pay in the census or tax, they should pay all this to the part of the churches at all times.

Comeatus, the reporter, recognized the advice of Radleici and subscribed.

Dated on the 3rd of July in the year of Christ the propitiation of the thirteenth reign of lord Louis, the most glorious king in eastern France, by the indictment of the seventh; the act of the Frankfurt palace region; in the name of God, happily, amen.

LETTER IX

In the holy and individual name of the Trinity. King Louis II, by divine favor. It is worth it... Comeatus reporter recognized the advice of Radlaic.

Dated the 4th day of January in the year of Christ, propitiating the 13th reign of Lord Louis, the most serene king in eastern France, indictment 9. Acts of the city of Regensburg; in the name of God, happily, amen. King Louis grants to Briwin a hundred manors by the river Valchau.

LETTER X

In the name of the holy and individual trinity. Louis, by the divine grace of the king... the venerable man Erchamfridus, bishop of the church of Regensburg, presented to our obtues a certain tradition, that for the love of God and for the cure of his soul, Count William had surrendered to the monastery of St. Hemmeram all his property, which he seemed to have below the two rivers, that is, between Agast and Nardina, from the places where they flow into the Danube, to the places where they are diverted from the veins into the rivers, and so up to the Nortuualt in this part of the forest without the conclusion of the boundary, with the remaining houses and buildings and the manors and the remaining meadows, pastures, forests and waters water, moving and immobile streams, cultivated or uncultivated, whatever he had, even those things which Engilrade had allowed his wife to have during the days of her life, so that after his death it would be clear that they belonged to the same tradition of St. Hemmeram, moreover, and whatever Rosdorf seemed to have of all things on that side of the Danube, whatever belonged to him in manors and buildings and vineyards, whether cultivated or uncultivated, he delivered and fully delegated to the holy place already mentioned. But for complete firmness and security, the mentioned Bishop Erchamfrid and our relative asked our highness that we should confirm the same tradition by our precept of meekness. We did not want to deny the petition, but as to each of our faithful who justly asked, let the greatness of all our faithful know that we have granted them and confirmed them in everything. For this reason we have decided to make these points of our serenity around the monastery itself, by which we order and command that all the things which the aforesaid Count William had delivered and consigned should be established forever through this authority of ours at the aforesaid holy place, even by decreeing [or] we firmly command, that all the men who are known to command over the same things and seem to belong to the aforesaid monastery, both Bavarii and Selau, free and serfs, and to have previously ceased to exist by giving them to the master, no public judge nor any power dares to constrain them in anything, but neither presumes to abstract their cause nor urges them to go to the wing; but let the governors and ministers and advocates of the same seat lawfully possess and govern the above-mentioned things, and at all times stand fully under our protection and immunity. But if there should be anyone who wishes to demand or exact some of the justices written above against these men, then the advocates and ministers of the monastery should, as is just, endeavor diligently to inquire into the real truth and correct it. In the same way we command and command in every way that no public judge or (anyone) from judicial power over the things that belong to Erlafa and in Herilungeuelde and not to Sirnicha and around Agasta or Bernsnicha and Rostorf or the below mentioned boundaries and markame where the things of Saint Peter and the saints of Hemmeram are known to belong, and he has no power over free men or Selaui to separate them, but he does not at any time appeal to any plea or to go to the enemy, as long as they wish to do justice to the advocates of the same seat; but, as we have said, with all integrity the aforesaid things shall in the future be under our defense and protection of immunity without the slightest contradiction or complication...

I recognized and subscribed to the notice of the Radleic council.

Dated on the 15th of the month of February in the year of Christ propitiation of the 20th reign of Lord Louis, the most serene king in eastern France, the first indictment; act of the city of Regensburg; in the name of God, happily, amen.

LETTER XI

In the name of the holy and individual trinity. King Louis, by the divine favor of clemency... a certain man named Otgarius, whom we have decided to be the abbot of the monastery named Altaha, which is consecrated in honor of St. Maurice the martyr of Christ, offered to our obituaries not only the authority of the immunity of the blessed memory of Charles, our ancestor the most august emperor , but he also showed the letters of Thassilon, a former leader in the duchy of Bauaricus, on the same subject, in which it was contained, that the aforesaid monastery under his name and defense, with the cells and places subject to it, things or men, and all things belonging to it, was at present strongly fortified and defended from the restlessness of the judicial power would have been Wherefore also, for the firmness of the matter, the aforesaid man suggested to our clemency, that, following the manner of our fathers or predecessors of our kings, that is to say, following the precept of this kind of our immunity, for the love of God and the reverence of the holy place itself, we should command to enlist around the monastery itself. To whose request we gladly acceded to this precept of our immunity towards the monastery itself, for the sake of protection and defense, and for the love of divine worship, as well as for the remedy of our souls. present as well as future, neither counts nor centurions nor executors in churches or places or fields or other possessions, which in modern times in any villages or territories under the control of our kingdom he justly and legally holds and owns, even those which in the right of the monastery itself divine piety will increase , to hear cases, or to exact taxes and tributes, or to remove guarantors, or men of the monastery, both innocent and servants, commanding slaves and servants over his land, neither justly or unjustly severing them, and making no returns or lodgings, or making ready, or seeking illicit opportunities, nor entering into our future times. let him not presume to demand at any time the things which have been mentioned above; but let the aforesaid man and his successors have the possessions of the aforesaid monastery, with all things subject to him, and men both innocent and servants, of whatever nation they may be, and all those belonging to him or looking after him, under the protection and immunity of our defense, removed from the restlessness of the entire judicial power and popular appeal, in a quiet order and to possess quiet security, and the advocates of the peace of the church themselves will decide and finish every case to be investigated and discussed...

Hadebert the subdeacon recognized and (subscribed) the advice of Grimold the arch-chaplain.

Dated on the 11th of the month of May in the 25th year of the reign of Louis, the most serene king, reigning in eastern France, indictment V; act in the town of Potamo; in the name of God, happily, amen.

LETTER XII

In the name of the holy and individual trinity. Louis, by the grace of God, the king... we were given to one of our primates named Ratbotus half of one treasury called Tullina, situated in the region of Pannonia, with all the appurtenances, that is to say, those belonging to the treasury itself, as well as pasture lands for slaves and vineyards, and the rest that may be mentioned or mentioned they can, we have contributed to his own, on that account if he had kept his faith towards us inviolable. But he who alienated himself from us with all his might, and defrauded our faith and oath by all unfaithfulness, pleased our serenity to receive the same half of the mentioned treasure for our dominion, and for the divine absolution of the memory of our ancestors, namely the most august emperors, and for the remedy of our souls and the salvation of our bodies to Saint Hemmeramm to contradict and to confirm. That the greatness of all our faithful may know that we have done this by our authority, in such a way that the very half of the treasury should serve the table of the monks at the table of the lord of the feast there, and no bishop or any prelate presumes to give the same things as a benefit to anyone or to receive them for his own work. but let them serve only for their work, and let our bearer Rathbodon have the same half of the aforesaid treasury as long as we are able to help him to another place from other things; and then, at the same moment of time, the aforesaid monks should receive the aforesaid half of the treasury, together with all that is consistent above, let them hold and possess, and whatever they choose to do for their own benefit, they should have the free and most secure power to do it all at the mercy of Christ...

Eberhard, the notary, recognized and signed the advice of Vitgarius the chancellor.

Dated on the 15th of the month of May, in the 27th year of the reign of Louis, the most serene king, reigning in eastern France, indictment 7. The act of the Frankfurt palace region; in the name of God, happily. Amen.

LETTER XIII

In the holy and individual name of the Trinity, Louis, divine favoring grace king... our venerable bishop Hardvuicus, coming to the presence of our nobles, demanded our serenity, so that we had granted ten manors of our property to our faithful Albric and his choir bishop, consistent between Raba and Chuomberch. Having willingly agreed to his request for his love and service, we gave him the aforesaid ten manors at Nuzpach with the buildings above them and the fields and pastures, forests, water and streams in the prescribed ten manors, which lie within the alode of Amalgeri and Valtilon and at Odinburch and places. where the mountains begin to rise, and so into the common forest, for that reason we hand over and transfer to the right and dominion of the prescribed chorbishop Albric the ten manors prescribed by law and our dominion, so that whatever from this day onwards the chorbishop Albricus prescribed from the prescribed 10 mansas, whom he prayed it is our majesty and those whom we have granted to him, whatever he chooses to do, he has the power to do whatever he chooses, without any disturbance, but with the help of God, for ever and ever, without any contradiction...

Eberhard, the reporter, recognized the advice of Vuitgarius.

Dated on the 8th of October in the year Christ propitiation of the 28th reign of Lord Louis the Most Serene King reigning in eastern France, indictment 8. Acts of Hostermontingon royal town; in the name of God, happily, amen.

LETTER XIV

In the name of the holy and individual trinity. King Louis II by divine favor. For if we endeavor to fulfill those things which the faithful of our kingdom have begged of us for their opportunities, we not only fulfill the royal custom decently, we also undoubtedly make them more faithful and devoted in our service, and we clearly believe that it will be beneficial for them to attain eternal life happily. Therefore let him find out the skill of all our loyalists, that is to say, present and future, as Briuuinus, our faithful leader, coming to the presence of our nobles, demanded our serenity, so that of the things of his property, which we had conceded to him as property, he might give some portion in memory of Elus to St. Maurice and to our monastery of Altaha, of which at that time Otgarius the abbot seemed to be in charge and rector. Having willingly agreed to the request, we decided to do so. Briuumus, our faithful leader, with our consent and permission, gave to the aforesaid monastery of St. Maurice, the martyr of Christ, from his property in his leadership, whatever he had to the Salabiugites below these boundaries: to the east beyond the river Sala as far as Slougenzinmarcham and Stresmaren and so up through Balam as far as Waltungesbah and so from there to Hrabagiskeit and to Chirihstetm. Afterwards, however, the aforesaid faithful abbot

Our Otgarius implored our majesty to confirm the same things by the precept of our authority. Just as the aforesaid terms have been defined in the aforesaid places, so henceforth to the aforesaid monastery, by this precept of our authority, the matter itself shall consist in perpetual times with no disturbance, but with the help of God. And in order that this authority of our bounty may be more firmly established, and in future times be more truly believed and more diligently observed by our faithful, we have confirmed it with our own hand under it and ordered it to be strengthened with the impression of our ring, the Sign of the Most Serene King Louis.

Ebarhardus, the reporter, recognized the advice of Uulitgar and went down.

Dated on the 10th of march in the year of Christ propitiation of the 28th reign of the lord Louis, the most serene king reigning in eastern France, by the indictment of the 8th; the act of Regensburg as a royal city; in the name of God, happily, Amen.

LETTER XV

In the name of the holy and individual trinity. Louis, by the divine grace of the king... our venerable archbishop Adalwinus, coming to the presence of our nobles, requested our serenity, that, as a reward for our increase, certain things of our property should be given to the holy church of Inuauense, which was built in honor of St. Peter, the prince of the apostles, and St. Robert, where he also rests in body, and the aforesaid venerable bishop himself presides, we would have granted him to remain perpetually in his own right. To whose request, for the love of our Lord Jesus Christ, or for the reparation of the souls of our ancestors, and of the blessed memory of our lord and father, and of our own, we have willingly agreed to grant an increase in wages. We deliver therefore to the aforesaid house of God the city of Sabaria and Peinihaa, just as our count Odolricus and sent about the same things surrounded them with the rest of our faithful and clothed the aforesaid venerable archbishop about the same things, so from now on we will by law forever that they remain at the aforesaid house of God. In addition, we also hand over to our own those courts which were previously there for the benefit of someone given, either on our part or on the part of any other person, whose names are these: ad Magalicha, ad Uuahauua. to Liupina, to Holunburc, to Tmgisimas, to Penninuanc, to the church of Anzon, to Uuitanespere, to the church of Ellodis, to the church of Minigoni the priest, to Kundpoldesdori, to Rapa, to dry Sabaria, also to Pemicahu, to Salapiugin and the church to Chuartinahu, the church to Kensi, the church to Ternperch, the church to Gundoldi, the church to Sabniza, to Nezilnpah, likewise to Rapa, to Tuddleipin, to Sulpa, to Labant, to Kuroiza the benefice of Engilbald, to Carantana the church of St. Mary, to Trahoue, to Gurniz, to Trebina, to Astaruuiza, to Friesah, to Crazulpa, to Pelisa, to Chumbenza, to Undrima, to Iestinich, to Prucca, to Moriza, to Strazinolun two places, to Luminich near Rapa, that is to say that from this day onwards the aforesaid things to the aforesaid the house of St. Peter and St. Robert, where he also rules in body, may they continue by law forever without any contradiction... Hebarhard the notary recognized the advice of Grimaldi's archchaplain and went under.

Dated on the 12th of the month of December in the year of Christ's propitiation of the 28th reign of the lord Hludouicus, the most serene king reigning in eastern France, indictment 8. Acts of Matahhoua royal town, happily given. Amen.

LETTER XVI

In the name of the holy and individual trinity. Louis, by the divine grace of the king... our venerable abbot Otgarius addressed our highness, humbly imploring, that we had granted certain things of our property to the monastery called Althaha, built in honor of St. Maurice, as our own. We therefore willingly agreed to his request and granted certain things of our property to the monastery of Althaha, that is, a town called Nabawmida near the river Trebina. The aforesaid abbot also reminded our highness how our lord Charles, our grandfather, gives permission to his faithful to seize and inherit the property of the churches of God in Pannonia, which is known to have been done by his permission in many places and also to this monastery. For there were certain places in the vestibule of the aforesaid monastery called Scalcobah, just as the river itself went to the western side as far as Dagodeosmarcha and from there to the eastern side as far as Ruzaramarcha, and to a place called Cidalaribah in the pass of the river Enisa, which lies between the Danube and Ibiza and Hurula in the southern part up to the top of the mountain, and to the Biuginmanso, and whatever pertains to the aforesaid towns, that is, in the manors' buildings, cultivated land and uncultivated vineyards, meadows, forests, hunting pastures, watercourses. Although, therefore, the aforesaid things had been in the clothing of the prescribed monastery, they were not confirmed by the precept of any authority. When reminded of this matter, we ordered these to become the tips of our authority...

Ebarhardus, the reporter, recognized Grimaldi's approach to the archchapel and went down.

Dated the 16th of July in the year Christ propitiation of the 31st reign of the lord Louis, the most serene king reigning in eastern France, by the indictment of the 10th; the act of Hostermontinga, the royal town; happily in the name of God. Amen.

LETTER XVII

In the holy and individual name of the Trinity. Louis, by the divine favor of the king ... we, for the increase of our wages and for the reparation of the souls of our grandfather and father, and also at the request of Adelwin, the venerable archbishop of the church of St. Juvavense, have granted certain things of our property to St. Robert consisting in Pannonia, that is, to Labenza, to Wisitindorf of the land set up, ready for plowing, whole manors, that is to each colony 90 acres and of the forest on each side in the circle and in all parts one thousand, with lands of meadows and pastures and watercourses going out and coming back, the whole and to the whole of our right and dominion into the right and dominion of St. Robert we hand over and transfer to the church of Saint Juvavense, that is to say that from this day and onward things are prescribed to the aforesaid place by this precept of our authority fully confirmed in the name of God with no one disturbing but God helping may they continue for ever and ever without any modesty or restlessness... Hebarhardus, the notary, recognized Grimaldi's advice and signed it.

Dated on the 6th of October, in the propitious year of Christ, of the 33rd reign of Louis the Most Serene King, reigning in the east of France, by the 13th indictment; act of Mattahhove; in del name happily amen.

LATIN TEXT

EPISTULA I

In nomine Domini Dei et Salvatoris nostri Jesu Christi: Ludwicus et Lothaius divina ordinante providentia Imperatores Augusti. Si erga loca divimo cultui mancipata imperiali more beneficia largimur opportuna, id nobis procul dubio ad stabilitatem imperii nostri et animae salutem proficere minime dubitamus. Igitur notum esse volumus cunctis fidelibus sanctae Dei ecclesiae et nostris, praesentibus scilicet et futuris, quia ad deprecationem dilecti filii nostri Ludwici Regis Waioariorum et Geroldi comitis concessimus cuidam monasterio nostro, cujus vocabulum est Chremisa, quod est constructum in honore et veneratione Domini et Salvatoris nostri Jesu Christi situm in pago Trungowe, ubi praesenti tempore vir venerabilis Sigehardus abba praeest, et monachis ibidem per tempora: degentibus quoddam territorium, quod est in pago Grunzwiti juxta montem Sumerberch, quod usque modo servi vel Sclavi ejusdem monasterii ad censum tenuerunt, qui ad partem comitis solvebatur, ubi etiam monachi de praefato monasterio ecclesiam et domoset caetera aedificia construxerunt. Quod territorium ita terminatur. Incipit enim ex plaga orientali a Sumerperoch, sicut missi Geroldi comitis designaverunt, usque in Draeisma ad locum, qui vocatur Hohoga Plaettchinn, et inde sursum usque ad territorium episcopatus Pataviensis ecclesiae et exinde ad plagam australem usque in Heribrunnum. Deinde ex parte occidentali usque ad eum locum, ubi Flinspach exit de sylva a parte aquilonis, sicut ipsa sylva pergit usque ad jam dictum montem, qui vocatur Sumerperch. `

Memoratum vero territorium, quantumcumque infra suprascriptam terminationem consistit, salvis tamen proprietatibus liberorum Sclavorum, reliquum quidquid infra has terminationes praesenti tempore ad partem comitum pertinebat, omnia supradicto monasterio Chremisae per hanc nostram auctoritatem praesentialiter tradimus et de nostro jure in jus et dominationem ejus transfundimus ita videlicet, ut quidquid de praefatis territoriis ob utilitatem et profectum praesoripti monasterii rectores et ministri ejus facere vel judicare voluerint, libero in omnibus potiantur arbitrio faciendi, quidquid elegerint. Et ut haec auctoritas nostris futurisque temporibus domino protegente valeat inconvulsa manere, manibus propriis subterfirmavimus et anuli nostri impressione signari jussimus...

Durandus diaconus ad vicem Fridagisi recognovi. Datum XI. kal. april. Anno Christo propitio XV. Imperii Domini Ludowici serenissimi Imperatoris et Lotharii VI. Indictione VI. Actum Aquisgrani Palatio regio in Dei nomine feliciter. Amen.

EPISTULA II

In nomine domini nostri Jesu Christi dei omnipotentis. Hludouuicus divina largiente gratia rex Baioariorum. ...vir venerabilis Gauzbaldus sacri palatii nostri summus cappellanus et abba monasterii quod dicitur Altaha, quod est constructum in honore sancti Mauricii martyris Christi, adiens excellentiam nostram innotuit clementie nostre, qualiter postquam terra Auarorum ex parte ab avo nostro domno Karolo imperatore capta fuisset, ipsius permissu atque consensu quedam res in ipsa marcha ad ius regium pertinentes eidem monasterio conlate fuissent, quas etiam usque nunc predictum possedit monasterium. Sed qula auctoritas traditionis exinde minime apparebat, deprecatus est idem Gauzbaldus abba, ut nostre auctoritatis largitionem atque confirmationem eidem daremus monasterio, per quam ipsas res in postmodum predictum monasterium eiusque rectores absque cuiuslibet inpedimento aut contradictione tenere et dominare potuisset. Cuius deprecationem propter divinum amorem et reverentiam ipsius sancti loci libenter annuimus et ipsas res perpetuo possidendas sollemni datione eidem concessimus monasterio, id est locum qui nuncupatur Uuahouua, qui terminatur a fonte rivoli qui vocatur Mustrica usque in eum locum, ubi ipse Danubium influit, ac deinde tendit sursum in ripam Danubii usque in Bohbab, et ultra Bohbah mansum unum, et inde iuxta Bohbah sursum usque in verticem montis qui nuncupatur Ahornico, nec non et alium locum nuncupantem Accussabah iuxta ripam Danubii, cuius mensura est in longitudine miliarium uňum et similiter in latitudine, nee non et campum unum, qui continet mansum unum, quem interiacet causa Frisingensis ecclesiae. Has itaque res cum mancipiis domibus edificiis vineis terris silvis pratis pascuis aquis aquarumve de cursibus, quantumcumque infra predicta terminia de eisdem rebus continetur, totum et ad integrum in jus et dominationem prediote ecclesiae perpetualiter ad habendum conferimus; ita videlicet ut quicquid de ipsis vel in ipsis rectores et mimistri supramemorate sedis ob utilitatem et commoditatem ipsius ecclesiae facere vel iudicare voluerint, liberam in omnibus habeant potestatem faciendi quicquid elegerint...

Adalleodus diaconus advicem Gauzbaldi recognovi.

Data pridie non. octobr. anno Christo propitio XVII imperii domni Hludouuici serenissimi augusti et anno V regni nostri, indictione VII. actum Ragenesburg civitate; in del nomine feliciter amen.

EPISTULA III

In nomine domini nostri Iesu Christi dei omnipotentis. Hludouuicus divina largiente gratia rex Baioariorum... nos pro mercedis nostrae augmento concessimus sanctae Reginesburgensi[s] ecclesiae quae est constructa in honore sancti Petri principis apostolorum et sancti Emmerammi, ubi etiam idem beatissimus martyr Christi corpore quiescit humatus, cui praesenti tempore venerabilis vir Baturicus episcopus auctore deo praeesse videtur, quasdam res proprietatis nostrae, quae sunt in provintia Auarorum, id est locum, ubi antiguitus castrum fuit gui dicitur Herlungoburg, cum religuis adiacentiis in circuitu, quarum terminia sunt ab eo loco, ubi Erlafa in Danubium cadit, sursum per ripam eiusdem fluminis usque ad locum qui dicitur Erdgastegi, et ab eodem flumine in orientali parte usque in medium montem qui apud Uuinades Colomezza vocatur, ubi in duabus arboribus evidentia signa monstrantur, etab eo loco in parte aquilonis usque in Danubium et ad meridiem et occidentem per verticem montis, sicut evidentia arborum signa demonstrant, usque ad supradictum locum Erdgastegi. Has itaque res cum Seclavis ibidem commanentibus cum domibus aedificiis terris cultis et incultis pratis pascuis silvis aquis aquarumve decursibus adiacentiis perviis exitibus et regressibus, quantumcumque infra praedicta terminia continentur, totum et ad integrum praedictae ecclesiae perpetuo ad habendum concessimus et de nostro iure in ius et dominationem eius liberalitatis nostrae munere contulimus, ita videlicet ut quicquid ab hodierno die et tempore de praedictis rebus et mancipiis rectores et ministri memoratae sedis ob utilitatem et commoditatem eiusdem ecclesiae facere vel iudicare voluerint, libero m omnibus perfruantur arbitrio faciendi quicquid elegerint...

Adalleodus diaconus advicem Gauzbaldi recognovi et subscripsi.

Data II non. octubr. anno XVIIII imperii domni Hludouuici serenissimi augusti et anno VII regni nostri, indictione XI; actum Reginesburg civitate; in dei nomine feliciter amen.

EPISTULA IV

In nomine domini nostri Iesu Christi dei omnipotentis. Hludovuicus divina largiente gratia rex Baioariorum... nos pro mercedis nostre augmento concessimus ecelesie Patauiensi, gue est constructa in honore sancti Stephani protomartiris, ubi etiam sanctus Valentinus confessor Christi corpore requiescit, cui presenti tempore venerabilis vir Reginarius episcopus preesse videtur, quasdam res proprietatis nostre, gue sunt in provintia Auarorum in loco gui dicitur Litaha super fontem gui vocatur Sconibrunno, quas olim Theodericus habult in sua potestate. Has itaque res, sicut diximus, cum casis domibus terris cultis et mcultis pratis silvis pascuis aquis aquarumve decursibus adiacentus perviis exitibus et regressibus totum et ad integrum, quemadmodum predictus Theodericus eas habuit in potestate, ita predicte ęcclesie presentaliter concessimus et de nostro iure in ius et dominationem eius liberalitatis nostre munere conferimus, ita videlicet ut quicquid rectores et ministri supradicte sedis de ipsis rebus iure ecclesiastico facere voluerint, libero in omnibus perfruantur arbitrio faciendi, tantum scilicet ut dum Anno corepiscopus atque Anno nepos eius advixerint, ipsas res tenere et usare faciant et nullus eis ipsas abstrahere presumat et post illorum discessum cum integritate ad eandem ecelesiam revertantur...

Adalleodus diaconus advicem Gauzbaldi recognovi.

Data ITII non. mar. anno XX imperii domni Lůdovuici serenissimi augusti et anno VII regni nostri, indictione XI; actum Ostrehoua palatio nostro; m dei nomine feliciter amen.

EPISTULA V

n nomine sanctae et individuae trinitatis. Hludouuicus divina favente gratia rex... nos pro mercedis nostrae augmento concessimus ecclesiae Patauensi[s], quae est constructa in honore sancti Stephani protomartyris, ubi etiam sanctus Ualentinus confessor Christi corpore requiescit, cui praesenti tempore venerabilis vir Reginarius episcopus praeesse videtur, quasdam res proprietatis nostrae, quae sunt in provintia Auarorum in loco qui dicitur Kirichbach, id est ecclesiam unam constructam cum territorio ad mansos centum faciendum et plus, quarum terminia sunt ab ipso loco pergens per unam semitam usque ad locum qui dicitur (Tumulus) et inde per circuitum usque ad praedictum Kirichbach et inde usgue ad markam Theotheril et inde usque sursum Cumenberg. Has itaque res cum praedicta ecclesia cum vineis terris cultis et incultis pratis silvis pascuis aquis aquarumve decursibus adiacentiis perviis exitibus et regressibus totum et ad integrum, quemadmodum Ratbodus comes Annoni corepiscopo ipsas res consignavit, ita praedictae ecclesiae praesentaliter concessimus et de nostro jure in ius et dominationem eius liberalitatis nostrae munere conferimus, ita videlicet ut quicquid rectores et ministri supradictae sedis de ipsis rebus iure ecclesiastico facere voluerint, libero in omnibus perfruantur arbitrio faciendi, tantum scilicet ut dum Anno corepiscopus atque Anno nepos eius advixerint, ipsas res tenere et usare faciant et nullus eis ipsas abstraere praesumat et post illorum discessum cum integritate ad eandem ecclesiam revertantur.

Adalieodus diaconus advicem Grimaldi recognovi et subscripsi.

Data XIIII kalendas mar. anno Christo propitio tertio regni domni Hludouuici regis in orientali Francia, indictione XILI; actum Ostrenhoua" palatio regio; in dei nomine feliciter amen.

EPISTULA VI

In nomine sancte et individue trinitatis. Lödewicus divina favente gracia rex... Nos pro mercedis nostre augmento concessimus ecclesie Juuauensi, que constructa est in honore sancti Petri principis apostolorum, ubi eciam sanctus Rědbertus confessor Christi corpore quiescit humatus, cui presenti tempore venerabilis vir Liuprammus archiepiscopus auctore deo preesse videtur, quoddam territorium in Sclauinia im loco nuncupante Ipusa iuxta Ipusa fumen—ex utraque parte ipsius fluminis terminatur ab occidentali parte, quod Theodisca lingua wagreini dicitur, usque in orientalem partem ad unum parvum rivulum, ab aguilonal parte de illa publica strata usque m mediam eilvam. Hoc itaque territorium cum soclesia, quam dudum Adalrammus quondam secundum nostram licenciam ibidem edificavit, cum campis silvis pratis pascuis aquis aguarumve decursibus mobile et immobile, guemadmodum infra predicta terminia continetur, totum et ad integrum prefate ecclesie concessimus... ita videlicet ut quicquid exinde rectores et ministri supramemorate sedis ob utilitatem et comoditatem ipsius ecclesie facere vel iudicare voluerint, libero... perfruantur arbitrio faciendi quicquid elegerint...

Adalleodus diaconus advicem Grimaldi recognovi et subscripsi.

Data VIIIT kal. octobr. anno Christo propicio quarto regni domni Lódewici regis in orientali Francia, indictione XV; actum Ohoberg; in dei nomine feliciter amen.

EPISTULA VII

In nomine sanctae et individuae trinitatis. Hludouuicus divina favente gratia rex ... nos depraecantibus fidelibus nostris Baturico venerabili episcopo, Uuermhario comite, Baboni comite, ut aliquas res proprietatis nostrae cuidam presbitero nomine Dominicus ad proprium concedere disposuissemus, quod ita et fecimus, in loco qui dicitur ad Brunnaron, quod circumcapiebat Ratpero clericus tuxta rivolum qui vocatur Seuira in marca, ubi Radpoti et Rihharu comitatus confiniunt, interè silvis campis pratis pascuis aquis aquarumve decursibus vel quicquid memoratus Ratpero clericus circumcapiebat, eidem presbitero Dominico ob elemosinam nostram ad proprium concessimus...

Reginbertus subdiaconus advicem Radlaici recognovi et subscripsi.

Actum ad Rotachin XVII kal. octobr. anno Christo propitio XII regni domni Hludouuici regis in orienti Francia; in dei nomine feliciter amen.

EPISTULA VIII

In nomine sanctae et individuae trinitatis. Hludouuicus divina favente gratia rex... vir venerabilis Gozbaldus Uuirziburgensis ecclesiae episcopus ad nostram veniens praesentiam praesentavit obtutibus nostris quoddam. praeceptum domni ac genitoris nostri pie recordationis Hludouuici serenissimi augusti, in qua continebatur, qualiter dive memoriae domnus Karolus atque avus noster prestantissimus imperator antecessoribus suis Bereuuelpho et Liudrido et Egiluuardo nec non et Uuolfgario episcopis praecepisset, ut in terra Sclauorum, qui sedent inter Moinum et Radantiam fluvios, qui vocantur Moinuuinidi et Ratanzuurmnidi, una cum comitibus, qui super eosdem Sclauos constituti erant, procurassent, ut inibi sicut in ceteris cristianorum locis ecclesiae construerentur, quatenus ille populus noviter ad cristianitatem conversus habere potuisset, ubi et baptismum perciperet et praedicationem audiret et ubi inter eos sicut inter ceteros cristianos divinum officium celebrari potuisset; et ita a memoratis episcopis et comitibus, gui tam temporis eidem populo praepositi fuerant, adserit esse conpletum et ecolesias quattuordecim ibi fuisse constructas. Insuper domnus ac genitor noster piissimus imperator... ad praefatas basilicas dotandas, quae, ut diximus, iussu et consilio domm Karoli sive avi nostri in terra praedictorum Sclauorum a memoratis episcopis constructae sunt in eodem pago, tradidit de rebus suis propriis ad unamquamqe mansos duos cum supersedentibus duobus tributarus excepto illo manso, super quem primitus unaquaeque earundem ecclesiarum aedificata est, pleniter in perpetuum habere concessit atque inviolabiliter confirmavit, eo videlicet modo ut quicquid idem tributari in censu vel tributo solvere debent, hoc totum ad partem earundem ecclesiarum omni tempore persolvant...

Comeatus notarius advicem Radleici recognovi et (subsoripsl).

Data III non. iul. anno Christo propitio XIII regni domni Hludouuici gloriosissimi regis in orientali Francia, indictione VII; actum Franconofurt palatio regio; in dei nomine feliciter amen.

EPISTULA IX

In nomine sancte et individue trinitatis. Hludouuicus divina favente gratia rex. Dignum est... Comeatus notarius advicem Radlaici recognovi.

Data IIII idus ianuarias anno Christo propitio XIII regno domni Hludouuici serenissimi regis in orientali Francia, indictione IX; actum Reganesburg civitate; in dei nomine feliciter amen. Ludovicus rex concedit pleno iure Briwino centum mansos iuxta fluvium Valchau.

EPISTULA X

In nomine sanctae et individuae trinitatis. Hludouuicus divina favente gratia rex... vir venerabilis Erchamfridus Reganesburgensis ecclesiae episcopus obtulit obtutibus nostris quandam traditionem, quod Uuilihelmus comes ob dei amorem et animae suae remedium ad monasterium sancti Hemmerammi tradiderat omnem proprietatem suam, quod ille habere videbatur infra duo flumina, id est inter Agastam et Nardinam, a locis videlicet ubi ipsa in Danubium fluùnt, usque ad loca, ubi de venis in amnes dirivantur, et ita usque in Nortuualt in hane partem silve sine termini conclusione, cum domibus et aedifciis reliquis et mancipiis atque manentibus pratis pascuis silvis aquis aquarumve, decursibus mobilibus et inmobilibus cultis vel incultis quicquid habuit, etiam et res ilas, quas Engilrade coniugi suae ad dies vitae suae habere concesserat, ut post obitum illius ad eandem traditionem sancti Hemmerammi pertinere constaret, insuper et quiequid ad Rosdorf habere videbatur, omnia et ex omnibus rebus ex illa parte Danubii quicquid sibi pertinebant in mancipiis et aedificiis ac vineis cultis vel incultis, totum et integrum ad iam dictum" sanctum locum tradidit atque pleniter delegavit. Sed pro integra firmitate ac securitatis studio memoratus Erchamfridus episcopus atque familiaris noster petiit celsitudinem nostram, ut eandem traditionem per nostrum mansuetudinis praeceptum confirmare deberemus. Culus petitioni denegare noluimus, sed sicut unicuique fidelium nostrorum iuste petentium ita nos illi concessisse atque in omnibus confirmasse omnium fidelium nostrorum cognoscat magnitudo. Propterea hos apices serenitatis nostrae circa ipsum monasterium fieri decrevimus, per quos praecipimus atque iubemus, ut omnes res, quas praedictus comes Uuilihelmus tradiderat atque consignaverat, per hanc nostram auctoritatem ad iam dictum sanctum locum in perpetuum consistant, etiam statuentes [seu] firmiter iubemus, ut omnes homines, qui super easdem res commanere noscuntur et ad praefatum monasterium pertinere videntur tam Baioarii quamque Selau, liberi et servi, et inantea consistere? domino donante potuermt, nullus iudex publicus neque ulla potestas eos in quoquam constringere audeat, sed neque illorum causam abstrahere presumat nec in alam partem ire conpellat; sed liceat rectoribus et ministris et advocatis ejusdem sedis res superius nominatas legaliter possidere ac regere et omni tempore sub nostra defensione atque immunitatis tuitione pleniter consistere. Si vero aliquis fuerit, qui contra istos homines superius conscriptos aliquas iustitias requirere aut exactare voluerit, tune advocati et ministri ipsius monasteri illud, prout iustum est, diligenter rel veritatem inquirere studeant et emendent. Similiter quoque praecipimus atque omnimodis iubemus, ut nullus iudex publicus neque (quislibet) ex iudiciaria potestate super rebus, quae pertinent ad Erlafa et in Herilungeuelde nec non et ad Sirnicha et circa Agasta seu Bernsnicha atque Rostorf vel infra praedicta terminia et markame ubi res sancti Petri et sancti Hemmerammi noscuntur pertinere, neque super hominibus liberis vel Selauis ullam potestatem habeat m guoguam illos distringendos, sed neque ad placitum ullum vel in hostem ullo umquam tempore ire conpellat, quamdiu advocatis eiusdem sedis iustitiam facere voluerint; sed, sicut diximus, cum omni integritate praenominatas res in futurum sub nostra defensione et inmunitatis tuitione absque alicutus contrarietate aut inpedimento consistant...

Comeatus notarius advicem Radleic recognovi et subscripti.

Data XV kalend. febroarias anno Christo propitio XX regni domni Hludouuici serenissimi regis in orientali Francia, indictione prima; actum Reganesburg civitate; in dei nomine feliciter amen.

EPISTULA XI

In nomine sanctae et individuae trinitatis. Hludouuicus divina favente clementia rex.... vir quidam nomine Otgarius, quem nos quidem ad monasterium nomine Altaha, quod in honore sancti Mauricii martyris Christi est consecratum, abbatem esse statuimus, obtulit obtutibus nostris non solum auctoritatem emunitatis beatae memoriae Karoli avi nostri augustissimi imperatoris, sed et Thassilonis quondam ducis in ducatu Bauarico super eadem re litteras ostendit, in quibus continebatur insertum, quod praefatum monasterium sub suo nomine et defensione cum cellulis et locis sibi subiectis rebus vel hominibus et omnibus ilhe pertinentibus actenus ab inquietudine judiciariae potestatis munitum atque defensum firmissime fuisset. Unde etiam pro rei firmitate suggessit vir praenominatus clementiae nostrae, ut paternum seu predecessorum nostrorum regum videlicet morem sequentes huiuscemodi nostrae emunitatis praeceptum ob amorem dei et reverentiam ipsius sancti loci circa ipsum monasterium conscribere iuberemus. Cuius petitioni libenter adguiescentes hoc emunitatis nostrae praeceptum erga ipsum monasterjum gratia tuitionis et defensionis ac pro divini cultus amore nec non animae nostrae remedio consoribi decrevimus, per quod firmiter et omnimodis imperamus, ut nullus iudex puplicus vel quislibet ex iudiciaria potestate aut ullus ex fidelibus nostris tam praesentibus quam et futuris neque comites neque centenaru neque exactores in ecclesias aut loca vel agros seu reliquas possessiones, quas moderno tempore in quibuslibet pagis yel territoriis infra ditionem regni nostri iuste et legaliter tenet ac possidet yel etiam ea, quae in iure ipsiusmonasterii voluerit divina pietas augeri, ad causas audiendas vel freda et tributa exigenda aut fideiussores tollendos aut homines ipsius monasterii tam ingenuos quam servos, Sclauos et accolas super terram ipsius commanentes nec iuste nec iniuste distringendos et nullas reddibitiones vel mansiones aut paratas faciendas aut inlicitas occasiones requirendas nostris nec futuris temporibus ingredi audeat nec ea, quae supra commemorata sunt, nullo umquam tempore exigere přaesumat; sed liceat memorato viro suisque successoribus res praedicti monasterii cum omnibus rebus sibi subiectis et hominibus tam ingenuis quam servis, cujuscumque sint nationis, atque omnibus ad se pertinentibus vel aspitientibus sub tuitionis atque emunitatis nostrae defensione, remota totius iudiciariae potestatis inquietudine et vulgari appellatione, quieto ordine ac tranquilla securitate possidere, et advocati paus ecclesiae omnem causam inguirendam et discutiendam ipsi diiudicent et finiant...

Hadebertus subdiaconus advicem Grimoldi archicappellani recognovi et (subscripsi).

Data XI kal. mai. anno XXV regni Hludouuici serenissimi regis in orientali Frantia regnante, indictione V; actum in villa Potamo; in dei nomine feliciter amen.

EPISTULA XII

In nomine sanctae et individuae trinitatis. Hludouuicus divina favente gratia rex... nos cuidam ex primatibus nostris nomine Ratboto medietatem unius fisci qui vocatur Tullina, situs in regione Pannonia cum omnibus appendiciis elus, videlicet qui ad ipsum fiscum pertinent, tam mancipiis quam vineis terris pascuis et cetera quae dici aut nominari possunt, in proprium contulimus, ea ratione si fidem suam erga nos inviolatam servasset. Sed qula ipse a nobis totis viribus se alienavit et fidem atque iusiurandum omni infidelitate fraudavit, placuit serenitati nostrae eandem medietatem memorati fisci ad nostram dominationem recipere atque pro absolutione divine recordationis antecessorum nostrorum, augustissimorum scilicet imperatorum et pro remedio animae nostrae et corporis salvatione ad sanctum Hemmerammum contradere atque confirmare. Quod ita per hanc nostram auctoritatem nos fecisse omnium fidelium nostrorum magnitudo cognoscat, ea ratione ut ipsa medietas ipsius fisci ad mensam monachorum ibi domino famulantium ibi iugiter deserviat, et nullus episcopus aut guislibet praelatus easdem res in beneficium alicui dare sive ad opus suum recipere praesumat, sed solummodo ad opus ipsorum deserviant, et tamdiu eandem medietatem praenominati fisci Ratbodonem infertorem nostrum habere liceat, quousque nos in alterum locum ex aliis rebus illum adiuvare possimus; atque tunc eodem momento temporis memorati monachi praefatam medietatem fisci cum omnibus supra consistentibus recipiant teneant atque possideant et quicquid exinde pro utilitate sua facere voluerint, liberam et firmissimam im omnibus habeant potestatem Christo propitio faciendi...

Euerhardus notarius advicem Uuitgarii cancellarii recognovi et subscripsi.

Data kal. ma. anno XXVII regni Hludouuici serenissimi regis in orientali Francia regnante, indictione VII; actum Franconouurt palatio regio; in dei nomine feliciter amen.

EPISTULA XIII

In nomine sancte et individue trinitatis. Lůdovuicvs divina favente gratia rex... venerabilis episcopus noster Hardvuicus veniens in procerum nostrorum presentiam postulavit serenitatem nostram, ut de rebus proprietatis nostre X mansos Albrico fideli nostro suoque choriepiscopo concessissemus consistentes inter Raba et Chuomberch. Cuius peticioni ob amorem et servitium suum libenti animo assensum prebentes dedimus ei predictos mansos X ad Nuzpach cum edificiis desuper positis et campis et pratis pascuis silvis aquis aquarumve decursibus in prescriptis X mansis, qui coniacent intra alode Amalgeri et Vualtiloni et ad Odinburch atque ad loca, ubi montana incipiunt extolli, et sic in communem silvam, ea videlicet ratione ex iure et dominatione nostra prescriptos X mansos in ius et dominationem prescripti Albrici choriepiscopi tradimus atque transfundimus, ut quicquid ab hodierna die et deinceps prescriptus choriepiscopus Albricus de prescriptis X mansis, quos deprecatus est celsitudinem nostram et quos ei concessimus, facere voluerit, nullo inquietante sed deo auxiliante perpetuis temporibus potestatem habeat faciendi quiequid elegerit absque alicuius contradictione...

Heberhardus notarius advicem Vuitgarii recognovi.

Data VIII kal. oct. anno Christo propitio XXVIII regni domni Lůdovuici serenissimi regis in orientali Francia regnante, indictione VIII; actum Hostermontingon villa regia; in dei nomine feliciter amen.

EPISTULA XIV

In nomine sanctae et individuae trinitatis. Hludouuicus divina favente gratia rex. Si enim ea, quae fideles regni nostri pro eorum oportunitatibus nos deprecati fuerint, implere studnuerimus, non solum regium morem decenter implemus, veram etiam eos procul dubio fideliores ac devotiores in nostro efficimus servitio er ad aeternam vitam feliciter optinendam profuturum liquido credimus. Quapropter comperiat omnium fidehum nostrorum presentium scilicet et futurorum sollertia, qualiter Briuuinus fidelis dux noster veniens in procerum nostrorum praesentiam postulavit serenitatem nostram, ut de rebus proprietatis suae, quas el in proprietatem concessimus, liceret el partem aliquam ob memoriam elus dare ad sanctum Mauricium et ad monasterium nostrum Altaha, cui tempore illo Otgarius abba praeesse videbatur et rector. Culus petitioni libenti animo assensum prebentes decrevimus ita fieri. Dedit itaque Briuumus fidelis dux noster cum consensu et licentia nostra ad praefatum monasterium sancti Mauricii martyris Christi de sua proprietate in suo ducatu quicquid habuit ad Salabiugiti infra terminos istos: in orientem ultra Salam fluviolum usque in Slougenzinmarcham et Stresmaren et sic sursum per Balam usque ad Uualtungesbah et sic inde usque in Hrabagiskeit et ad Chirihstetm. Postea vero praedictus fidelis abba

noster Otgarius deprecatus est celsitudienem nostram, ut easdem res per nostrae auctoritatis praeceptum confirmassemus, Cuius petitioni ob honorem dei et sancti Mauricii militis Christi et bonum illius servitium libenti animo assensum prebuimus et hoc ei nostrae auctoritatis praeceptum fieri iussimus, per quod decernimus atque iubemus, ut sicut praedicti termini in praedictis locis diffiniti sunt, ita deinceps ad iam dictum monasterium per hoc nostrae auctoritatis praeceptum Ipsae res nullo inquietante sed deo auxiliante perpetuis temporibus consistant in proprium. Et ut haec auctoritas largitionis nostrae firmior habeatur et per futura tempora a fidelibus nostris verius credatur et diligentius observetur, manu propria nostra subter eam firmavimus et anuli nostri inpressione roborare iussimus, Signum Hludouuici serenissimi regis.

Hebarhardus notarius advicem Uulitgari recognovi et subseripsi.

Data X kal. marcias anno Christo propitio XXVIII regni domni Hludouuici serenissimi regis in oriental Frantia regnante, indictione VIII; actum Reganesburc civitate regia; in dei nomine feliciter Amen.

EPISTULA XV

In nomine sanctae et individuae trinitatis. Hludouuicus divina favente gratia rex... venerabilis archiepiscopus noster Adaluuinus veniens in procerum nostrorum praesentiam postulavit serenitatem nostram, ut ob mercedis nostrae augmentum quasdam res proprietatis nostrae ad sanctam ecclesiam Inuauensem, quae est constructa in -honore sancti Petri principis apostolorum et sancti Rotberti, ubi etiam corpore requiescit et ipse praedictus venerabilis episcopus praeest, in proprium iure perpetuo permanendum concedissemus. Cuius petitioni ob amorem domini nostri Jesu Christi seu ob remedium animarum antecessorum nostrorum ac beatae memoriae domni ac genitoris nostri nostraeque etiam mercedis augmentum libenti animo assensum prebentes decrevimus ita fieri. Tradimus itaque ad praedictam casam dei Sabariam civitatem et Peinihhaa, sicut Odolricus comes noster et missus de ipsis rebus eas circuivit ceterigue nostri fideles et praedictum venerabilem archiepiscopum de ipsis rebus vestivit, ita deinceps iure perpetuo volumus, ut ad praedictam casam dei permaneant. Insuper etiam tradimus ibi istas curtes in proprium, quae antea ibi in beneficium fuerunt ex alicuius dato sive ex parte nostra sive ex alterius cuiuslibet parte ibi antea beneficiatae fuissent, quarum haec sunt nomina: ad Magalicham, ad Uuahauua,. ad Liupinam, ad Holunburc, ad Tmgisimam, ad Penninuuanc, ad ecclesiam Anzonis, ad Uuitanespere, ad ecclesiam Ellodis, ad ecclesiam Minigonis presbiteri, ad Kundpoldesdorí, ad Rapam, ad siccam Sabariam, item ad Pemicahu, ad Salapiugin et ecclesiam ad Chuartinahu, ecclesiam ad Kensi, ecclesiam ad Ternperch, ecclesiam Gundoldi, ecclesiam ad Sabnizam, ad Nezilnpah, item ad Rapam, ad Tuddleipin, ad Sulpam, ad Labantam, ad Kuroizam beneficium Engilbaldi, ad Čarantanam ecclesiam sanctae Mariae, ad Trahoue, ad Gurniz, ad Trebinam, ad Astaruuizam, ad Friesah, ad Crazulpam, ad Pelisam, ad Chumbenzam, ad Undrimam, ad Iiestinicham, ad Pruccam, ad Morizam, ad Strazinolun duo loca, ad Luminicham iuxta Rapam, ea videlicet ratione ut ab hodierna die et deinceps praedictae res ad praedictam casam sancti Petri et sancti Rotberti, ubi etiam ipse corpore regulescit, iure perpetuo permaneant absque alicuius contradictione... Hebarhardus notarius advicem Grimaldi archicappellani recognovi et subseripsi.

Data XII kal. decemb. anno Christo propitio XXVIII regni domni Hludouuici serenissimi regis in orientali Francia regnante, . indictione VIII; actum Matahhoua villa regia; in del nomine feliciter Amen.

EPISTULA XVI

In nomine sanctae et individuae trinitatis. Hludouuicus divina favente gratia rex... venerabilis abba noster Otgarius adīt celsitudinem nostram humiliter implorans, ut quasdam res proprietatis nostrae ad monasterium quod vocatur Althaha, constructum in honore sancti Mauricii, in proprium concedissemus. Nos itaque petitioni ipsius libenti animo assensum praebuimus et concessimus quasdam res proprietatis nostrae ad monasterium Althaha, id est villam quae vocatur Nabauumida iuxta rivulum Trebinam. Ammonuit etiam celsitudinem nostram praedictus abba, qualiter domnus avus noster Karolus licentiam tribuit suis fidelibus in augmentatione rerum ecclesiarum dei in Pannonia ca[r]pere ac possidere hereditatem, quod per licentiam ipsius in multis locis et ad istud etiam monasterium factum esse dinoscitur. Fuerunt namque in vestitura praedicti monasterii quaedam loca nomine Scalcobah, sicut ipse rivulus fiuit in occidentalem partem usque in Dagodeosmarcha et inde in orientalem plagam usque in Ruzaramarcha, atque in locum quem vocant Cidalaribah in saltu Enisae fluvi, qui coniacet inter Danubium et Ibisam atque Hurulam in meridianam partem usque in verticem montis, et ad Biugin mansos V, et quicquid ad praedictas villas pertinet, hoc est in mancipiis edificiis terris cultis et incultis vineis pratis silvis venationibus pascuis aquis aquarumve decursibus. Licet itaque fuissent in vestitura praedictae res ad praescriptum monasterium, tamen non ibl erant confirmatae per ullius auctoritatis praeceptum. Qua de re commoniti hos nostrae auctoritatis apices fieri iussimus ...

Hebarhardus notarius advicem Grimaldi archicappellani recognovi et subseripsi.

Data XVI kal. iul. anno Christo propitio XXXI regni domni Hludouuici serenissimi regis in orientali Francia regnante, indictione X; actum Hostermontinga villa regia; in dei nomine feliciter. Amen.

EPISTULA XVII

In nomine sancte et individue trinitatis. Lódewicus divina favente gratia rex ... nos ob nostre mercedis augmentum et pro remedio anime domni avi ac genitoris nostri nec non eciam pro peticione Adelwini sancte Iuuauensis ecclesie venerabilis archiepiscopi concessimus quasdam res proprietatis nostre ad sanctum Rödbertum> consistentes in Pannonia, id est ad Labenza, ad Wisitindorf de terra exartata, parata scilicet ad arandum, mansos integros VIII, id est ad unamquamque coloniam iugera XC et de silva undique in gyrum scilicet ac per omnes partes milarium unum, cum terris pratis pascuis aquis aquarumve decursibus exitibus et regressibus, totum et ad integrum ex iure et dommacione nostra in ius et dominacionem sancti Rödberti ad sanctam Iuuauensem ecclesiam tradimus atque transfundimus, ea videlicet racione ut ab hodierna die et deinceps prescripte res ad predictum locum per hoc nostre auctoritatis preceptum plenius in dei nomine confirmatum nullo inquietante sed deo auxiliante perpetuis temporibus permaneant absque ulla modestia vel inquietudine... Hebarhardus notarius advicem Grimaldi recognovi et subscripsi.

Data VI non. octobris anno Christo propicio XXXIII regnidomn Lodewici serenissimi regis in orientah Francia regnante, indictione XIII; actum Mattahhoue; in del nomine feliciter amen.

The Scriptorium Project is the work of a small group of lay people of various apostolic churches who are interested in the preservation, transmission, and translation of the works of the early and medieval church. Our efforts are to make the works of the church fathers accessible to anyone who might have an interest in Christian antiquities and the theological, philosophical, and moral writings that have become the bedrock of Western Civilization.

To-date, our releases have pulled from the Greek, Syriac, Georgian, Latin, Celtic, Ethiopian, and Coptic traditions of Christianity, and have been pulled from sundry local traditions and languages.

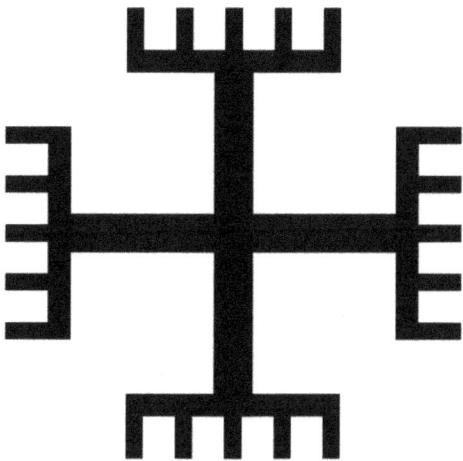

OTHER WORKS FROM THE WEST- & SOUTH SLAVIC COLLECTION:

PAX THORUN by *Wladyslaw II Jagiello, King of Poland* (June 2006)
THE ACT OF THE INCORPORATION OF PRUSSIA by *Casimir IV Jagiello, King of Poland* (July 2007)
EX COMMISSO NOBIS by *Pope Innocent II* (Oct. 2008)
INDUSTRIAE TUAE by *Pope John VIII* (Nov. 2008)
LETTER TO KING SVATOPLUK I, KING OF SLAVS by *Pope Stephen V*
PILLARS OF THE SLAVIC CHURCH by *Louis II the German* (Jan. 2009)
THREE LETTERS FROM THE COMPANION OF THE BULGARS by *St. Rupert of Juvavum* (Aug.2017)

www.ingramcontent.com/pod-product-compliance
Lightning Source LLC
LaVergne TN
LVHW061603070526
838199LV00077B/7159